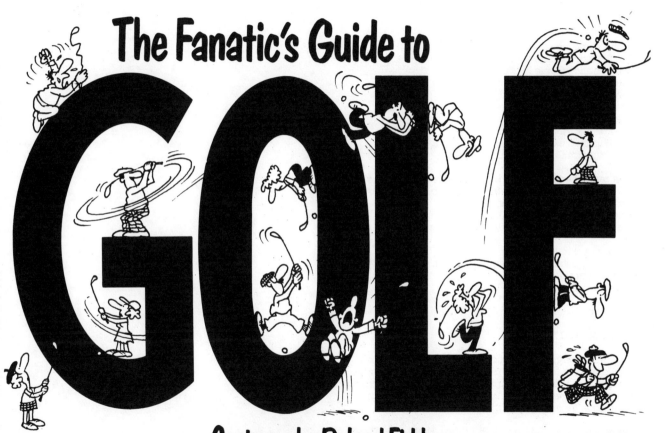

The Fanatic's Guide to GOLF

Cartoons by Roland Fiddy

In the same series:
The Fanatic's Guide to the Bed
The Fanatic's Guide to Cats
The Fanatic's Guide to Computers
The Fanatic's Guide to Dads
The Fanatic's Guide to Diets
The Fanatic's Guide to Dogs
The Fanatic's Guide to Husbands
The Fanatic's Guide to Sex
The Fanatic's Guide to Skiing

First published in the USA in 1992 by Exley Giftbooks
487 East Main Street, Suite 326, Mt. Kisco, NY 10549-0110.
Published in Great Britain in 1991 by
Exley Publications Ltd, 16 Chalk Hill,
Watford, Herts WD1 4BN, United Kingdom.

Second and third printings, 1989
Fourth, fifth, sixth and seventh printings, 1990
Eighth printing, 1991
Ninth and tenth printings, 1992

ISBN 1-85015-172-5

Typeset by Brush Off Studios, St Albans, Herts AL3 4PH
Printed in Spain by GRAFO, S.A. - Bilbao

Roland Fiddy

Roland Fiddy, Cartoonist.

Born in Plymouth, Devon. Studied art at Plymouth and Bristol Colleges of Art. Works as a freelance cartoonist and illustrator. His cartoons have been published in Britain, the United States, and many other countries. Has taken part in International Cartoon Festivals since 1984, and has won the following awards:

1984 Special Prize, Yomiuri Shimbun, Tokyo.
1984 First Prize, Beringen International Cartoon Exhibition, Belgium
1984 Prize of the Public, Netherlands Cartoon Festival.
1985 First Prize, Netherlands Cartoon Festival
1985 "Silver Hat" (Second Prize) Knokke-Heist International Cartoon Festival, Belgium.

1986 First Prize, Beringen International Cartoon Exhibition, Belgium
1986 First Prize, Netherlands Cartoon Festival
1986 First Prize, Sofia Cartoon Exhibition, Bulgaria.
1987 Second Prize, World Cartoon Gallery, Skopje, Yugoslavia.
1987 "Casino Prize" Knokke-Heist International Cartoon Festival, Belgium
1987 UNESCO Prize, Gabrovo International Cartoon Biennial, Bulgaria.
1987 First Prize, Piracicaba International Humour Exhibition, Brazil.
1988 "Golden Date" award, International Salon of Humour, Bordighera, Italy.
1988 Second Prize, Berol Cartoon Awards, London, England.
1989 E.E.C. Prize, European Cartoon Exhibition, Kruishoutem, Belgium.
1989 Press Prize, Gabrovo International Cartoon Biennial, Bulgaria.
1990 First Prize, Knokke-Heist International Cartoon Festival, Belgium.
1991 Highly Commended, XVI International Biennale of Humorous Art, Tolentino, Italy.

Golf: how it all began ...

2

... and how it continued.

Golf is not only recreational ...
... it is also useful.

The fanatical golfer addressing the ball.

The fanatical golfer should not worry about his standard of play, as this will affect his standard of play.

Nothing must interfere with his concentration.

The fanatical golfer never misses an opportunity to improve his...

... er – or her putting.

1   2   3

4   5   6

7

8

9

10

11

12

La Ronde

The fanatical golfer knows how important it is to present a brave face.

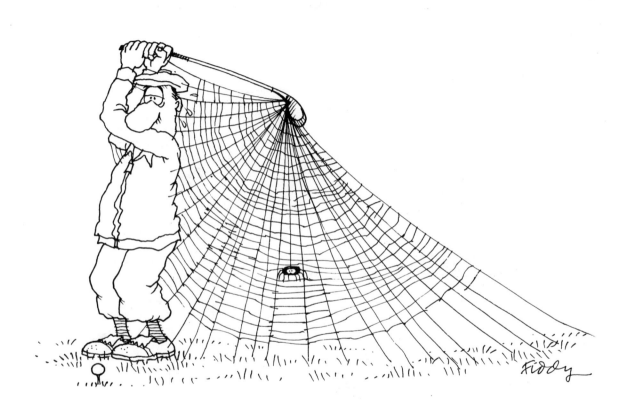

The fanatical golfer knows how important it is not to rush the back swing.

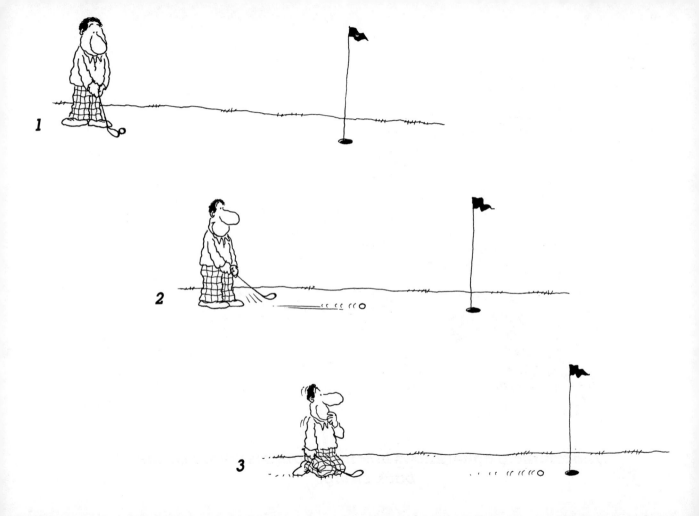

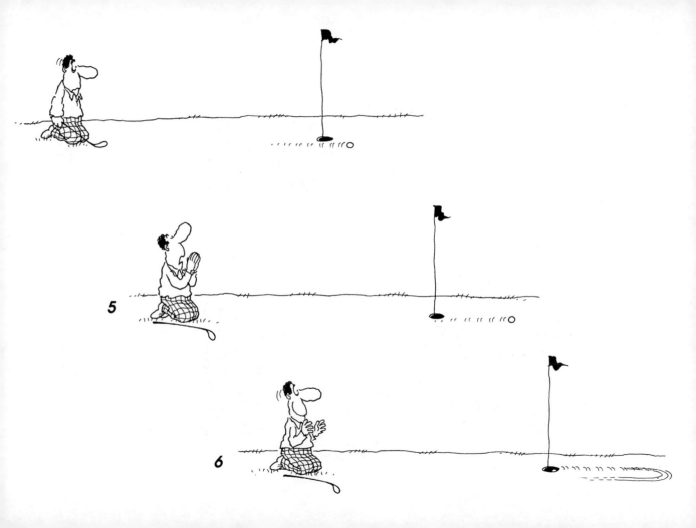

1

You must not carry more than fourteen clubs in your bag ...

2

... this is a sensible rule for obvious reasons.

Play the ball as it lies.

This is against the Rules ...

... and so is this.

Fanatical golfers need to be specially patient with beginners...

DAMMIT! I FORGOT TO WISH MURIEL A MERRY CHRISTMAS THIS MORNING!

"Old men forget; yet all shall be forgot,
But he'll remember with advantages,
What feats he did that day ..."
(Shakespeare: _Henry V_)

To the fanatical golfer, every difficult hole is another Everest to conquer.

The fanatical golfer finds it hard to accept criticism ...

... or to ignore it ...

but is willing to take constructive advice.

1

2

3

4

The fanatical golfer understands the importance ...

... of controlling one's temperament.

The game is full of surprises.

*Of course, not everybody appreciates golf –
some people think it's just a load of balls.*

The angler and the golfer swopping stories.

Golf: the ideal combination of recreation and exercise.

Cartoons by Roland Fiddy

The Crazy World series

There are now 20 different titles in this best-selling cartoon series – one of them must be right for a friend of yours....

    The Crazy World of Birdwatching (Peter Rigby)

    The Crazy World of Cats (Bill Stott)

    The Crazy World of Cricket (Bill Stott)

    The Crazy World of Gardening (Bill Stott)

    The Crazy World of Golf (Mike Scott)

    The Crazy World of the Handyman
      (Roland Fiddy)

    The Crazy World of Hospitals (Bill Stott)

    The Crazy World of Jogging (David Pye)

    The Crazy World of Love (Roland Fiddy)

    The Crazy World of Marriage (Bill Stott)

    The Crazy World of Music (Bill Stott)

    The Crazy World of the Office (Bill Stott)

    The Crazy World of Photography (Bill Stott)

    The Crazy World of the Royals (Barry Knowles)

    The Crazy World of Rugby (Bill Stott)

    The Crazy World of Sailing (Peter Rigby)

    The Crazy World of the School (Bill Stott)

    The Crazy World of Sex (David Pye)

    The Crazy World of Skiing
      (Craig Peterson & Jerry Emerson)

    The Crazy World of Tennis (Peter Rigby)

Great Britain: Order these super books from your local bookseller or from Exley Publications Ltd, 16 Chalk Hill, Watford, Herts WD1 4BN.